James E. Ritchie

The Cruise of the Elena

Or, yachting in the Hebrides

James E. Ritchie

The Cruise of the Elena
Or, yachting in the Hebrides

ISBN/EAN: 9783337312848

Printed in Europe, USA, Canada, Australia, Japan

Cover: Foto ©Andreas Hilbeck / pixelio.de

More available books at **www.hansebooks.com**

THE
CRUISE OF THE ELENA

OR

YACHTING IN THE HEBRIDES

BY

J. EWING RITCHIE

Author of "The Night Side of London," &c. &c.

London
JAMES CLARKE & CO., 13, FLEET STREET

1877

LONDON
W. SPEAIGHT & SONS, PRINTERS, FETTER LANE.

TO

JOHN ANDERSON, ESQ.,

OF GLEN TOWER, ARGYLESHIRE,

OWNER OF THE ELENA,

This Little Volume is Dedicated

BY THE AUTHOR,

IN MEMORY OF A PLEASANT CRUISE ON BOARD THE ELENA

IN THE AUTUMN OF 1876.

CONTENTS.

CHAPTER	PAGE
I.—Off for Greenock	1
II.—From Greenock to Ardrossan	15
III.—A Sunday at Oban	27
IV.—From Oban to Glencoe	37
V.—Off Mull	47
VI.—Fast Day at Portree	57
VII.—To Stornoway	71
VIII.—Kintyre and Campbeltown	81
IX.—Back Again	97

I.

OFF FOR GREENOCK.

CHAPTER I.

OFF FOR GREENOCK.

THE late—I had almost written the last—Imperial ruler of France was wont to say—indeed, it was his favourite maxim—"Everything comes to him who waits." It was not exactly true in his case. Just as he was to have placed himself at the head of his followers, and make his reappearance in France, and to have effaced the recollections of Sedan, Death, who waits for no one, who comes at the appointed time to all, put a stop to his career. Nevertheless, the saying is more or less true, and especially as regards my appearance on board the *Elena*. Whether my great great grandfather was a Viking or no, I am unable to say; all I know is, from my youth upwards I have longed for a yacht in which I could cruise at my own sweet will. I am no great hand at singing, but when I do sing it is always of a

> "Life on the ocean wave,
> A home on the rolling deep."

And thus it happened that, when an invitation was sent to me, just as I was on the point of giving up the ghost, in consequence of the heat of a London summer, to leave Fleet Street, and cruise among the Western Islands of Scotland, I accepted it, as the reader may well suppose, at once.

It is somewhat of a journey by the Midland night express from London to Greenock; but the journey is one well worth taking, even if, as in my case, you do not get a Pullman car, as that had been already filled, and was booked full, so the ticket manager said, for at any rate twelve days in advance. It is really interesting to see that express start. "It is an uncommon fine sight," said a man to me the other night, as he lit his pipe at the St. Pancras Station. "I always come here when I've done work; it is cheaper than a public-house." And so it is, and far better in awakening the intellect or stimulating the life. It is true I did not see the express start, as I happened to be in it; but I had another and a greater pleasure—that of being whirled along the country, from one great city or hive of industry to another, till I found myself early in the morning looking down from the heights of Greenock on the busy Clyde below. It was a grand panorama, not easily to be forgotten. All at once it opens on you, and you enjoy the view all the more as it comes in so unexpected a manner.

Let me pause, and say a good word for the line that bears me swiftly and safely and pleasantly on.

The story of railway enterprise as connected with the Midland Railway has been told in a very bulky volume by Mr. J. Williams. I learn from it that forty years have elapsed since, originating in the necessity of a few coal-owners, it has gradually stretched out its iron arms till its ramifications are to be found in all parts of the land. Actually, up to the present time it has involved an expenditure of fifty millions, and its annual revenue reaches five. Daily—hourly, it rushes, with its heavy load of tourists, or holiday-makers, or men of business, past the ancient manor-houses of Wingfield, Haddon, and Rousbery; the abbeys of St. Albans, Leicester, Newstead, Kirkstall, Beauchief, and Evesham; the castles of Someries, Skipton, Sandal, Berkeley, Tamworth, Hay, Clifford, Codnor, Ashby, Nottingham, Leicester, Lincoln, and Newark; the battle-fields of St.

Albans, Bosworth, Wakefield, Tewkesbury, and Evesham.

But it is to that part of the line between Carlisle and Settle that I would more particularly refer—that boon to the southern tourist who, as the writer did, takes his seat in a Midland carriage at St. Pancras, and finds himself, without a change of carriage, the next morning at Greenock in time for the far-famed breakfasts on board the *Iona*. The ordinary traveller has no idea of the difficulties which at one time lay between him and his journey's end. "It is a very rare thing," once said Mr. Allport, the great Midland Railway manager, a name honoured everywhere, "for me to go down to Carlisle without being turned out twice. Then, although some of the largest towns in England are upon the Midland system, there is no through carriage to Edinburgh, unless we occasionally have a family going down, and then we make an especial arrangement, and apply for a special carriage to go through. We have applied in vain for through carriages to Scotland over and over again." And so the Midland had no alternative but to have a line of their own. When it was known at Appleby that their Bill had passed the Commons, the church bells were rung, and, as was quaintly remarked, the people wrote to the newspapers, and did all that was proper under the circumstances. No wonder Appleby rejoiced and was glad; for, though the county town of Westmoreland, it is not much of a place after all, and the railway must have been a boon to the natives—especially to the ladies, who otherwise, it is to be feared, would have wasted their sweetness on the desert air.

On Monday, the 2nd of August, 1875, after an expenditure of three millions, the Settle and Carlisle line was opened for goods traffic. It must have been an awful undertaking, the making of it. "I declare," said a rhetorical farmer, "there is not a level piece of ground big enough to build a house upon all the way between Settle and Carlisle." An ascent had to be made to a height of more than a thousand feet above the level of the sea, by an incline that should be easy enough for the swiftest passenger expresses and for the heaviest mineral trains to pass securely and punctually up and down, not only in the light days of summer, but in the darkest and "greasiest" December nights. To construct it the men had to cut the boulder clay—very unpleasant stuff to deal with—to hew through granite, to build on morasses and dismal swamps. Near the southernmost end of the valley, watered by the roaring Ribble, the town of Settle stands among wooded hills, overhung by a lofty limestone rock called Castlebar; while far beyond on the left and right rise, above the sea of mountains, the mighty outlines of Whernside and Pennegent, often hid in the dark clouds of trailing mists. Up the valley the new line runs, pursuing its way among perhaps the loneliest dales, the wildest mountain wastes, and the scantiest population of any part of England. Three miles from Settle we reach Stainforth Force, and just beyond are the remains of a Roman camp. At Batty Green the navvies declared that they were in one of the wildest, windiest, coldest, and dreariest localities in the world. In the old coaching days the journey across these wilds was most disagreeable and trying. It was no unusual thing, we read, for rain to come down upon the travellers in torrents; for snow to fall in darkened flakes or driving showers of powdered ice; for winds to blow and howl with hurricane force, bewildering to man and beast; for frost to bite and benumb both hands and face till feeling was almost gone; and for hail and sleet to blind the traveller's eyes and to make his face smart as if beaten with a myriad of slender cords. In Dent Dale, which is almost ten miles in length, the scenery is remarkably fine. Nearly five hundred feet below, now sparkling in the sunlight, now losing itself among some clusters of trees, winds the river Dee; while first on one side and then on the other is the road that leads to Sedbergh. Leaving the tunnel, we find ourselves in Garsdale, in a milder clime and amidst more attractive scenery. Some four hundred feet below us the river may be observed winding over its rocky bed in the direction of Sedbergh, while we get extensive views on the west. Presently we see the Moorside Inn, a far-famed hostelry abounding in mountain dew, standing at the head of the valleys—the Wensleydale, winding eastward towards Hawes; the Garsdale Valley, going westward towards Sedbergh; and the Mallerstang, leading northwards towards Kirkby Stephen.

At Ais Gill Moor the line attains its highest altitude, 1,167 feet above the sea, from whence it falls uninterruptedly down to Carlisle. The country here is very wild and rugged. Stone walls mark the division of the properties, and scarcely any house can be seen. On the west the grandly impressive form of Wild Boar Fell rises. Still higher on the east is Mallerstang Edge. In the winter you can well believe that along this valley sweeps the wind in bitter blasts. Three miles after we have left the Moor Loch we are in Cumberland, and are reminded of other days when all the old manor-houses and other edifices were built for defence against the invasions of the Picts. Though the upper part of the Eden valley is now occupied by a few industrious farmers and peaceful shepherds, we instinctively think of the time when the slogan of border chiefs and their clansmen sent a thrill of terror through Mallerstang, and when sword and fire did terrible work to man and beast. Here is Wild Boar Fell, where, says tradition, the last wild boar was killed by one of the Musgrave family; and there in a narrow dale, overlooked by mountains and washed by the Eden, are the crumbling ruins of a square tower —all, alas! that remains of Pendragon Castle. About a mile before we come to Kirkby Stephen we pass on our right Wharton Hall, the seat of the now extinct dukes of that name. Near the town are two objects of especial interest—the

Ewbank Scar and Stenkrith Falls. The sight from Ormside Viaduct is wonderfully fine. Appleby, as seen from the line, has a very pleasing appearance. The railway runs past Eden Hall, the residence of Sir Richard Musgrave, the chief of the clan of that name. At the summit of a hill, near the Eden Lacy Viaduct, we find the remains of a Druid's temple, known by the name of "Long Meg and her Daughters." Close by is Lazonby, a village in the midst of interesting historical associations. As we pass through the ancient forest, we would fain stop and linger, as the scenery about here is deeply romantic, as much so as that of Derbyshire. At Armathwaite the beauty of the district culminates; and we gaze with rapture at its ancient quaint square castle, its picturesque viaduct of nine arches eighty feet high, its road bridge of freestone, its cataract, and its elm—said to be the finest in Cumberland. At Carlisle there is a fine railway hotel, which you enter by a side door from the platform, and where the traveller may attain such refreshment as he requires. Indeed, it is open to the public on the same reasonable terms as the London Tavern when it was the head-quarters of aldermanic turtle. The town is delightfully clean, and has many interesting associations; and as I stood upon the ramparts of the castle there on my return, smoking a cigar, there came to me memories of William Rufus, who built the wall, and planted in the town the industrious Flemings; of King David of Scotland; of Wallace, the Scottish hero, who quartered his troops there; of Cromwell, "our chief of men," as Milton calls him; and of the Pretenders, father and son. It is with interest I look at the church of St. Mary, remembering, as I do, that it was there Sir Walter Scott was married. I am told the interior of the cathedral is very beautiful, and crowded with memorials of a truly interesting character. Externally the place looks in good condition, as it was repaired as lately as 1853-6. Altogether the town appears comfortable, as it ought to do, considering it has extensive founderies and breweries, manufactories of woollen, linen, cotton, and other fabrics; communication with six lines of railway; a canal, two rivers, and two local newspapers. Nor is Carlisle ungrateful. I find in its market-place a statue to Lord Lonsdale, who has much property in these parts. One can tarry there long. Afar off you see the hills of the Lake

Country—the country of Southey and Wordsworth—and, if you but keep your seat, in an hour or two you may be, according to your taste, " touring it " in the land of Burns, or in the district immortalised by the genius of Sir Walter Scott.

As I went one way, and returned another, I enjoyed this privilege and pleasure. At Dumfries I could not but recollect that there the poet Burns wrote his

" Scots wha hae wi' Wallace bled;"

that there he died prematurely worn-out in 1796; that there, as he lay dying, the whole town was convulsed with grief; and that there his funeral was attended by some ten or twelve thousand of the people whose hearts he had touched, and who loved him, in spite of his errors, to the end. "Dumfries," wrote Allan Cunningham, " was like a besieged place. It was known he was dying, and the anxiety, not of the rich and learned, but of the mechanics and peasants, exceeded all belief. Wherever two or three people stood together, their talk was of Burns, and him alone. They spoke of his history, of his person, of his works, of his family, and of his untimely and approaching fate, with a warmth and enthusiasm which will ever endear Dumfries to my remembrance." Thinking of Burns, the time passed pleasantly, as I mused, half awake and half dreaming, that early summer morning, till I reached Greenock, where sleeps that Highland Mary, who died during their courtship, and of whom Burns wrote, in lines that will last as long as love, and woman, and the grave—

> "Ah! pale—pale now those rosy lips
> I aft hae kissed sae fondly;
> And closed for aye the sparkling glance
> That dwelt on me sae kindly.
> And mouldering now in silent dust
> That heart that loved me dearly;
> But still within my bosom's core
> Shall live my Highland Mary."

II.

FROM GREENOCK TO ARDROSSAN.

CHAPTER II.

FROM GREENOCK TO ARDROSSAN.

I SHALL never forget my first view of the Clyde from the heights above Greenock. It is true I had seen the Clyde before, but it was at Glasgow years ago, and it had left on my mind but a poor impression of its extent, or utility, or grandeur. What a sight you have of dockyards, where thousands of men are ship-building! and what a fleet of vessels laden with the produce of every country under heaven! As I take up a Scotch paper, I read:—"The cargoes imported during the month included 64 of grain, &c., 65 of sugar, 22 of timber, 5 of wine, 2 of fruits, 1 of brandy, 1 of ice, 3 of esparto grass and iron ore, 3 of rosin, 2 of oil, 1 of tar, 1 of guano, 1 of nitrate of soda, and 4 with minerals." And then how grand is the prospect beyond—of distant watering-places, crammed during the summer season, not alone with Glasgow and Edinburgh citizens, but with English tourists, who find in these picturesque spots a charm they can discover nowhere else. Almost all the way—at any rate, since I left Leeds—I have had my carriage almost entirely to myself; and now I am in a crowd greater and busier than of Cheapside at noon, with knapsacks and carpet-bags and umbrellas, all bent on seeing those beauties of Nature of which Scotland may well be proud.

To leave the train and hurry down the pier, and rush on board the *Iona*, is the work of a minute, but of a minute rich in marvels. The *Iona* is a fine saloon steamer, which waits for the train at Greenock, and thence careers along the Western Coast, leaving her passengers at various ports, and picking up others till some place or other, with a name which I can hardly pronounce, and certainly cannot spell, is reached. It must carry some fourteen or fifteen hundred people. I should think we had quite that number on board—people like myself, who had been travelling all night—people who had joined us at such places as Leicester, or Leeds, or Carlisle—people who had come all the way in her from Glasgow—people who had come on business—people who were bent on pleasure—

people who had never visited the Highlands before—people who are as familiar with them as I am with Cheapside or the Strand—people with every variety of costume, of both sexes and of all ages—people who differed on all subjects, but who agreed in this one faith, that to breakfast on board the *Iona* is one of the first duties of man, and one of the noblest of woman's rights. Oh, that breakfast! To do it justice requires an abler pen than mine. Never did I part with a florin—the sum charged for breakfast—with greater pleasure. We all know breakfasts are one of those things they manage well in Scotland, and the breakfast on board the *Iona* is the latest and most triumphant vindication of the fact. Cutlets of salmon fresh from the water, sausages of a tenderness and delicacy of which the benighted cockney who fills his paunch with the flabby and plethoric article sold under that title by the provision dealer can have no idea; coffee hot and aromatic, and suggestive of Araby the blest; marmalades of all kinds, with bread-and-butter and toast, all equally good, and served up by the cleanest and most civil of stewards. Sure never had any mother's son ever such a breakfast before. It was with something of regret that I left it, and that handsome saloon filled with happy faces and rejoicing hearts.

In about half-an-hour after leaving Greenock, I was at Kirn, a beautiful watering-place in Argyleshire, in one of the handsomest villas of which I was to find my host, and the owner of the *Elena*, one of the finest of the four or five hundred yachts which grace the lake-like waters of the Clyde, and which carry the ensign of the Royal Clyde Yacht Club. A volume might be written of the owner, whose place of business in Glasgow is one of the real wonders of that ancient town. Morrison, the founder of the Fore Street Warehouse, and the father of the late M.P. for Plymouth, was accustomed to say that he owed all his success in life to the realisation of the fact that the great art of mercantile traffic was to find out sellers rather than buyers; that if you bought cheap and satisfied yourself with a fair profit, buyers—the best sort of buyers, those who have money to buy with—would come of themselves. It is on this principle the owner of the *Elena* has acted. It is worth something to see the Sèvres china, the fine oil paintings, the spoils of such palaces as the Louvre or St. Cloud, the rarest ornaments of such exhibitions as those of

Vienna, all gathered together in the Glasgow Polytechnic, and to seek which the proprietor is always on the look-out, and to recollect that all this display has been got together by one individual, who began the world in a much smaller way, and who is still in the prime of life. A further interest attaches to the gentleman of whom I write, inasmuch as it was under his roof that the first article of the *Christian Cabinet*, swallowed up in the *Christian World*, was written. It may be to this it is due that at once I am at home with him, and that here on board the *Elena* we chat of what goes on in London as if we had known each other all our lives. By my side is his son-in-law—one of those well-trained, thoughtful divines who have left Scotland for the South, and who are doing so much to introduce into England that Presbyterianism the yoke of which our fathers could not bear, but on which we, their more liberal sons, have learned to look with a less jealous eye; and no wonder, for to know such a man as the Doctor is to love him. And now let me say a word as to the *Elena*, which is a picture to admire, as she floats calmly on the water, or speeds her way from one scene of Scottish story and romance to another. It is rarely one sees a yacht more tastefully fitted-up, and we have a ladies' drawing-room on board not unworthy of Belgravia itself. She is slightly rakish in build, but not disagreeably so. Her tonnage is 200 tons, and her crew consists, including the stoker and steward, of some eight clever-looking, sailor-like men. As we sleep on board I am glad of this. With Gonsalo I exclaim, "The wills above be done; but I had rather die a dry death."

And now, after skirting the greater and the lesser Cumbraes, and the cave where Bruce hid himself, &c., &c., we are coaling off Ardrossan, apparently a busy town on the Ayrshire coast. I have been on shore, and have seen no end of coal and lumber ships in the docks, and in the streets are many shops with all the latest novelties from town, and with ladies lounging in and out. I know I am in Scotland, as I hear the bagpipes droning in the distance, and stop to judge the beef and mutton exposed for sale at the shop of the nearest "flesher." On a hill behind me is a monument which, the natives inform me, is in memory of Dr. Mac-something, of whom I never heard, and respecting whom no one apparently can tell me anything. I know further I am in Scotland, as I see everywhere Presbyterian places of worship, and hear accents not familiar to an English ear. I know also I am in Scotland, as I see no gaudy public-house with superfine young ladies to attract my weak-kneed brethren to the bar, but instead dull and dark houses, in which only sots would care to go. I know I am in Scotland, because it is only there I read of "self-contained houses" to let or sell; and as to Ardrossan in particular, let me say that it is much frequented by the Glasgow merchants in the season; that it, with its neighbour Saltcoats, supports a *Herald*, published weekly for a penny; that from it, as a local poet writes—

"We see bold Arran's mountains gray,
In dark sublimity, stand forth in grandeur day by day."

The poet speaks truly. As I write I see the heights of the Scottish Alps, whose feet are fringed with the white villas of the Glasgow merchants for miles, and washed by the romantic waters of the Clyde.

Anciently Ardrossan was a hamlet of miserable huts, says Mr. Murray—Mr. Thomas, of Glasgow, not Mr. John, of London—gathered around an old castle on Castle Hill, the scene of some of Wallace's daring achievements, and destroyed by Cromwell. It was said to have belonged to a warlock, known as the Deil of Ardrossan. The present town was originated in 1806 as a seaport for Glasgow, but, like Port Glasgow, proved a failure in this respect. It is, however, generally well filled with shipping. The Pavilion, a residence of the Earl of Eglinton, adjoins the town. Steamers run thence to Belfast and Newry, and to Ayr and Arran and Glasgow.

Let me here remark, as indicating the cultivated character of the Scotchman, one is surprised at the number of local papers one sees in all the Scotch towns. They are mostly well written, and have a London Correspondent. It is beautiful to find how in the Scotch towns there is still faith left in the London Correspondent. The people swallow him as they do the Greater and Lesser Catechism, and even the London papers quote him as with happy audacity he describes the dissensions in the Cabinet—the hopes and fears of Earl Beaconsfield, the secret purposes of the garrulous Lord Derby, or the too amiable and communicative Marquis of Salisbury. When yachting I made a point to buy every Scotch paper I could, for the express purpose of reading what Our London Correspondent had got to say. I was both amused and edified. It is said you must go from home to hear the news. I realised that in Scotland as I had never done before. On the dull, wet days, when travelling was out of the question, what a boon was our "Own Special London Correspondent!"

III.

A SUNDAY AT OBAN.

CHAPTER III.

A SUNDAY AT OBAN.

TAKING advantage of a fine day, we left Ardrossan, with its coal and timber ships, early one Saturday, and were soon tossing up and down that troubled spot known as the Mull of Kintyre. It was a glorious sight, and one rarely enjoyed by tourists, who make a short cut across a canal, and lose a great deal in the way of beautiful effects of earth, and sea, and sky. On our left was the Irish coast, here but fifteen miles across, and far behind were the dark forms of the mountains of Arran. Islay, famed for its whisky in modern and for its romantic history in ancient times, next rises out of the waters. Jura, with its three Paps, as its hills are called, comes next, and then, in the narrow sound between Jura and Scarba, there is the terrible whirlpool of Corrybrechan, the noise and commotion of whose whirling waves are often, writes the local Guide-book, audible from the steamer. The tradition is, as referred to in Campbell's "Gertrude of Wyoming," that there a Danish prince, who was foolhardy enough to cast anchor in it, lost his life. To-day it is silent and at rest, and it requires some stretch of imagination to believe, as the poet tells us, that "on the shores of Argyleshire I have often listened with delight to the sound of the vortex at the distance of many leagues." At length we reach Scarba, Mull is swiftly gained, and there, on the other side of us, not, however, to be visited now, are Staffa and Iona. Altogether, we seem in a deserted district. It is only now and then we see a house, or gentleman's residence, and, except where we pass some slate works on our right, the rocks and hills around seem utterly unutilised. Occasionally we see a few sheep or cattle feeding, and once or twice we are cheered with arable land, and crops growing on it; but the rule is to leave Nature pretty much to herself. It is the same on the water. We on board the fairy *Elena*, and the gulls following in our wake, are almost entirely monarchs of all we survey. On we glide up the Frith of Lorne, which seems to narrow as we come near to Kerrera, which has on its lofty sea-cliff the ancient Castle of Glen; and there before us lies Oban, or the white bay, in all its charms of wood and hill and water. Oban is a growing place, and we land where the steamer which brings on the tourists from Iona has just put down its passengers, amongst whom I see Dr. Charles Mackay, who, in the evening of his days, much affects this delightful retreat—a place, I imagine, quiet enough in winter, but now seemingly the head-quarters of the human race. There are yachts all round, but none equalling the *Elena*. The hotels which line the bay are handsome, beautifully fitted up, and the proprietors are looking forward to the 12th of August and the advent of the English. All the shops are doing a roaring trade, and as to eggs, not one has been seen in Oban these four days. Here come the coaches, something of a cross between omnibuses and wagonettes, which run to Glencoe and Fort William, and other spots more or less famed in Scottish story; and here is the band to remind one of watering-places nearer home. I find here the original Christy's Minstrel (I never thought of finding him so far North), and the proprietor of an American bazaar, who tells me that he has been taking his £40 a night, but who finds himself too well known to the natives, and intimates that he will have to move off shortly; and last, but not least, a gentleman who modestly enters himself in the fashionable announcements as Smith, of London! I should like to see that Smith. I dare say I should know him; but at present I have not succeeded in running him down. If he is going to stay long at Oban, it strikes me he should have plenty of money in his pocket. I don't blame the Oban hotel-keepers. They have a very short summer, and are bound to make hay while the sun shines; but they do stick it on. The Doctor tells me of a Scotchman who came to London, and who, to illustrate the costliness of his visit, remarked to his friend that he had not been half-an-hour in the place but bang went sixpence. That economical Scot would find money go quite as quickly here. At any rate, such are my reflections as I turn into my little cot after, one by one, the lights in Oban have been put out, and the last of the pleasure-seekers has retired to roost.

On Sunday morning I wake to find that it has rained steadily all night, and that it is raining still. Mrs. Gamp intimates that life "is a wale o' tears." Oban seems to be such emphatically.

A Sunday at Oban.

This is awkward, as I hear the refined and accomplished lady who shares with us the perils and the dangers of the deep intimates that in Scotland people are not expected to laugh on the Sabbath-day. It rains all breakfast; it rains as we descend the *Elena's* side, and are rowed ashore; it rains as we make our way to the Established Church, in which that popular minister, the Rev. Mr. Barclay, of Greenock, is to preach. His sermon is on the death of Moses. He glides lightly over the subject, telling us that his text, which is Deut. xxxv. 5, teaches the incompetency of the noblest life, the penal consequences of sin, the mercy mingled with the Divine judgment, and the uniformity of God's method of dealing. Mr. Barclay is listened to with attention. In his black gown, his tall, dark figure looks well in the pulpit, and there must be some eight or nine hundred people present. There is a collection after, but I see no gold coin in the plate, though the bay is full of yachts, and there must be many wealthy people there. Perhaps, however, they patronise the small Episcopalian church close by. After the sermon, we are rowed back in the heavy rain to the yacht, and "it is regular Highland weather" is all the consolation that I get, as I dry myself in the stoke-hole, while the Doctor philosophically smokes.

In the evening we are rowed again on shore, and seek out the Free Church, where Professor Candlish, the son of the far-famed Doctor of that name, is to preach. He has the reputation of being a remarkably profound divine, and certainly reputation has not done him injustice in this respect. His sermon is a great contrast to that I heard in the morning. It is full fifty minutes long, and is an argumentative defence of the text, " Being justified freely by His grace through the redemption that is in Christ Jesus." The preacher proposed to deal with the objection, which he admitted might be fairly made, that if Jesus paid the debt, our salvation was not a matter of grace at all; and for this purpose we had line upon line in thoroughly old Scotch fashion, the hearers all the while looking out the passages of Scripture referred to in their Bibles. The sermon was old-fashioned as to thought, but the language was modern. I was glad I went to hear it. The congregation was not above half the size of that which appeared in the Established Church, and a great deal less fashionable. There you saw a good deal of the tourist element.

Here we had the real natives, as it were; and I must own that I saw more men than I should have seen in a congregation of the same size at home. At the church in the morning we had, in addition to the Scotch Psalms, such hymns as "I lay my sins on Jesus," and "Lord of the worlds above." In the evening we had no novelties of that kind. Indeed, the whole service was dry and severe to a degenerate Southern. Mr. Barclay quoted a good deal of Mrs. Alexander's fine poem on the death of Moses. Professor Candlish did nothing of the kind. His sermon was, in fact, quite in accordance with the day and the *genius loci*. I felt it was such a sermon as I had a right to expect. As I leave the church, I wonder to myself how the tourists manage. It is too wet to walk, and if they do take a walk it is not considered the correct thing in these northern latitudes, where, to make matters worse, the Sunday is nearly an hour longer than it is in London. I am afraid, however, some of the townsfolk find the time hang heavily on their hands. It seemed to me that there was an unusually large number of female faces at the window, and when the boat comes to fetch us on board the *Elena* all the windows are full of, I fear, frivolous spectators. It is true that I am adorned with a genuine Highland bonnet, and would make my fortune in London as a Guy on the fifth of November; but here Highland bonnets are common. It is true my companion is a great divine from town, and one well known in Exeter Hall; but here you would take him for a skipper, and nautical men are as common as Highland bonnets. I fear it is for very weariness that Oban ladies sit staring out of the windows on the empty streets and silent bay this dull and watery Sabbath night. I can almost fancy I hear them sing—

"I am a-weary, a-weary;
Oh! would that I were dead!"

IV.

FROM OBAN TO GLENCOE.

CHAPTER IV.

FROM OBAN TO GLENCOE.

A COUPLE of days' heavy rain quite exhausted the gaieties of Oban, and it was with no little pleasure that I heard the orders given to weigh the anchor and get up steam. I shed no tears as I saw the last of the long line of monster hotels, which rejoice when the Englishman, who has, perhaps, never been up St. Paul's, and who certainly has never visited Stratford-on-Avon, makes up his mind to turn his face northwards and do the Western Highlands and Islands of Scotland. I believe the hotels are excellent. I am sure one of them is—that kept by Mr. McArthur, who is an artist, and whose son, a little lad of ten years, paints in a way to remind one of similar achievements by Sir Thomas Lawrence; but it is much to be regretted that so many of the best spots for pleasant views above the town are marked off as private, and so shut out from the tourist altogether. As possibly these brief notes may be read in Oban, I refer to the fact, in order that the authorities of the place, ere it be too late, may be reminded of the impolicy of killing the goose for the sake of the eggs. There ought to be an abundance of pleasant walks and seats around Oban to tempt the tourist to linger there. It is related of Norman Macleod, as he stood on the esplanade, pointing to the town, the bay crowded with yachts, the Kerrera reflected on the sea as in a mirror, with the distant hills of Morven and Mull behind, that he exclaimed, " Where will you find in the whole world a scene so lovely as this?" and this was said after he had visited America, and India, and Palestine, and the whole continent of Europe. I am not prepared exactly to endorse that statement, but the language is natural to a Scotchman, who can see nowhere a land so romantic as his own. Oban, with its fine hotels on the front, with its beautiful bay, with its wooded or bare hills behind, looks well from the water; but nevertheless I had tired of it, after spending a couple of days contemplating its features from the deckhouse of the yacht, bathed as they were in what in London we should call unmitigated rain, but which here poetically is termed Scottish mist.

Well, as I have said, there was a shaking amongst the dry bones when it became known that the morning was bright and fine, or, in other words, that it did not rain. A noble peer, who had been shut up in his yacht two whole days, came up on deck and looked out. A great Birmingham man, anchored on the other side of us, hoisted his sails and cleared off. With the aid of the glass I could see the tourists turn out of the hotels, without mackintoshes and with umbrellas furled. Away flew the *Elena* past the ancient Castle of Dunollie, the seat in former ages of the powerful Lords of Lorn, and still the property of their lineal descendant, Colonel Macdougall. Rounding Dunollie Point, and passing the Maiden Island, the steamer enters on the broad waters of Loch Linnie, and here a magnificent scene opens on us. To the left are seen the lofty mountains of Mull, the Sound of Mull, the green hills of Morven, the rugged peaks of Kingairloch, and the low island of Lismore, where MacLean of Duart left his wife, a sister of the Earl of Argyll, to perish on a rock, whilst he pretended to solemnise her funeral with a coffin filled with stones. Fortunately, the lady was rescued, and the rest of the story may be read in Joanna Baillie's "Tragedy of Revenge." On our right stretches the picturesque coast of the mainland, revealing fresh beauties at every turn, with a splendid back-ground of towering mountains, such as the noble Ben Cruachan, who only a week since had his head covered with snow, and the rugged hills of Glen Etive and Glencreran. Lismore itself is well worthy of a short stay, as one of the earliest spots visited by the missionary, St. Maluag, from Iona, whose chair and well are yet shown. There are also in the island the remains of an ancient Scandinavian fortress, and many other objects of interest. We pass another old castle, that of Stalker, on a small island, a stronghold of the ancient and powerful Stewarts of Appin, who, though now extinct, anciently ruled over this region, and, connected with the royal family of that name, occupied a distinguished place in Scottish story. In the sunlight our trip is immensely enjoyable. The air has healing in its wings. You feel younger and lighter every mile. On the left are the splendid mountains of Kingairloch and Ardour, and on the right those of Appin and Glencoe. The view of the pass is very fine, and to enjoy it more we land at Ballachulish, and take such a drive as I may never hope to enjoy again. Ballachulish itself is an interesting place. Here a son of a King of Denmark was drowned, and at the adjacent slate quarry some six hundred men are employed at wages averaging about three pounds a-week. It is their dinner hour as we pass, and I am struck with the fineness of their *physique*. Though they speak mostly Gaelic, and are shut out from English literature, they must, from their appearance, be a decent set. In an English mining village of the same size I should see a Wesleyan and a Primitive Methodist Chapel, and a goodly array of public-houses and beer-shops. Here I see neither the one nor the other. At this end of the village is an Episcopalian place of worship, with its graveyard filled with slate stones. At the other end is the Free Church, and then, separated from it by a rocky stream, are the Established Church and the Roman Catholic Chapel. The village street is, I fancy, nearly a mile long, and the cottages, which are well built and whitewashed, seem to me crammed with children and poultry —the former, especially, very fine, with their unclad feet, and with hair streaming like that of Mr. Gray's bard. How they rush after our carriage like London arabs! I am sorry I don't carry coppers. Late as the season is, a few women are hay-making. What sunburnt, weather-beaten, wrinkled faces they have! Plump and buxom at eighteen, they are old women when they have reached twice that age.

As to Glencoe, what can I say of it that is not already recorded in the guide-books, and familiar to the reader of English history? The road is carried along the edge of Loch Leven, and is really romantic, with the rocks on one side, the winding glen in front, and the loch beneath. It is very narrow, and as we meet two four-horse cars returning with tourists we have scarce room to pass. Another inch would send us howling over into the loch below, but our steeds and our driver are trustworthy, and no such accident is to be feared. In the loch beneath we see St. Mungo's Isle, marked by the ruins of a chapel, and long used as a burial-place, the Lochaber people at one end, the Glencoe people at the other, as their dust may no more intermingle than may that of Churchmen and Dissenters in some parts of

England. A little further on is the gable wall, still standing, of the house of M'Ian, the unfortunate chief, who was shot down by his own fireside on that memorable morning of February, 1690. Is it for this the Glasgow people erected a statue to William III.? Further on we see the stones still remaining of what were once houses in which lived and loved fair women and brave men. One sickens now as we read the story of that atrocious massacre. A little more on our right is a rocky knoll, from which, it is said, the signal pistol-shot was fired. Happily, such atrocities are now out of date, but the blot remains to sully the fair fame of our great Protestant hero, and to stain to all eternity the memories of such men as Argyll and Stairs. Independently of the massacre, the spot is well worthy of a visit. There is no more rocky and weird a glen in all Scotland, and when the sun is hidden the aspect of the place is sombre in the extreme, and the further you advance the more does it become such. The larch and fir disappear from the sides of the hills, the river Coe dashes angrily and noisily at their feet, and before us is the waterfall which, here they tell us, was Ossian's shower-bath. Close by, Ossian himself is reported to have been born, and what more natural than that he should thus have utilised the stream? On the south is the mountain of Malmor, and to the north is the celebrated Car Fion, or the hill of Fingal. I gather a thistle as a souvenir of the place. Of course it is a Scotch thistle, therefore to be honoured, but for the credit of my native land, I must say it is a pigmy to such as I have seen within a dozen miles of St. Paul's. As a Saxon, I am especially interested in the horned sheep in these parts, which at first sight naturally you take for goats; with the Highland cattle, though by no means the fine specimens you see at the Agricultural Hall, and with the exquisite aroma (when taken in moderation) of the Ben Nevis "mountain dew." Returning, we pass the entrance to the Caledonian Canal—called by the natives the canawl—along which we were to have made our way to Nairn; but the *Elena* scorns the narrow confines of the canal, and claims to be a free rover of the sea.

V.

OFF MULL.

CHAPTER V.

OFF MULL.

As I sit musing in the dining-saloon of the *Elena*, it occurs to me that a Scotchman is bound to be a better educated man than an Englishman; for these simple reasons—in the first place, he does not drink beer—and beer is fatal to the intellect, inasmuch as it magnifies and fattens the body; and secondly, because the climate compels him to lead the life of a student. In the south, we Englishmen have fine weather. In this world everything is comparative. We in Middlesex may not have the warm sunshine and blue skies of France or Italy, but we have weather which admits of garden parties, and country sports, and pastimes; up in this region of mountain, rock, and river, it is perpetually blowing big guns or raining cats and dogs, and the Scotchman, as he can't go out, must sit at home and improve his mind. In dull weather Oban is not a lively spot, but here at Tobermory dulness fails adequately to express the thorough stagnation of the place. Few of my readers have ever heard of Tobermory; yet Tobermory is the principal town—indeed, the only one that is to be found in all Mull. It rose to its present height of greatness as far back as the year 1788, when it was developed under the auspices of the Society for the Encouragement of British Fisheries. But the place was founded before then, as three or four miles off there are the remains of a monastery, and in a niche in the wall of one of the hotels there was, evidently, a crucifix or an image of the Virgin Mary, whose name seems to be connected with the town. Tobermory means Well of St. Mary, and up at the top of the town there is shown to you the well of that name. The *Florida*, one of the ships of the Spanish Armada, was sunk off Tobermory, and some of her timbers and her brass and iron guns have occasionally been fished up. The place must be valuable, as the present proprietor gave £90,000 for the estate, which had been bought by the former owner for about a third of that sum. The house and ground are on the left, and his yacht lies in the bay as we enter. By our side are a few trading vessels which have entered the harbour for shelter. On the right, at the entrance of the harbour, is a rock, on which some one has had painted, in large red letters, "God is love." In rough seas, on this rock-bound coast, where the wind howls like a hurricane as it rushes down the gorges of the hills, and where the Atlantic seems to gather up its strength, here and there, at fitful intervals, ere it becomes still and tame—under the soothing influence of Scotch bag-pipes—it is well to remind the traveller on the deep that He, who holds the waters in the hollow of His hands, is love. Tobermory is, I imagine, a very religious place; on a Sunday night the Sheriff preaches in the Court House, and there, on our left, is a Baptist chapel—where, once upon a time, the Doctor preached, and in his warmth upset the candle over the head and shoulders of his colleague sitting below—and up on the hill is a kirk and a churchyard; the latter, as is the case with all the churchyards in this part of the world, in a truly disgraceful state of neglect, with the graves, which are but a few inches deep, covered with long grass and weeds. At one corner is what evidently was a receptacle for holy water, and all around the place there is an antiquity—in the grass growing in many of the streets, in the deserted walls of houses crumbling to decay, in the weather-beaten, ancient look of the people, certainly by no means suggestive of gaiety or life. Tobermory reminds me, says the Doctor, of what the auld woman said of the sermon—that it was neither amusing nor edifying. The Doctor's lady, overcome by her feelings, writes verses, which I transcribe for the benefit of my readers who may not enjoy the honour of her acquaintance.

> " Off Mull
> 'Tis rather dull.
> Hope is vain,
> Down pours the rain ;
> The wind howls
> Like groans of ghouls."

But the subject is too much for her, and we land to have a chat with the natives. A deal we get out of them, as we wander, something like the river of the poet—

> " Remote, unfriended, melancholy, slow."

They seem to me suspicious and reserved, as the Irishman when at home. We meet one of the natives—an ancient mariner, with a long, grey beard, and glistening eye. He can tell us all about the legends connected with the Well of St. Mary, we are told.

"You have lived here all your life?"

"Oh, yes," replies he, thoughtfully, picking the lower set of left grinders in his mouth.

"And you know the place well?"

"Oh, yes," says he, commencing picking on the other side of his mouth.

"And you can tell us all about it?"

"Oh, yes, sure," says he, as he calmly proceeds to pick the remainder of his teeth individually and collectively.

"What about the well—you know that?"

"Yes, it is up there," pointing to the spot we had just left.

"What do the people call it?"

"The Well of St. Mary."

"Can you tell us why?" said we, thinking that at last the secret which had been hidden from the policeman of the district and the inn-keeper (I beg his pardon, in these parts every little cabin in which you can buy whisky or get a crust of bread is an hotel), and every man we met. "Can you tell me why the place is so called?"

"Yes," says he, "the Well of St. Mary—that is the question." And then he shut up—the oracle was dumb. I need not describe my feelings of disappointment. I could have punched that man's head.

I learn that Mull is a cheap place—as it ought to be—to live in. In Tobermory, butter—beautiful in its way—is eighteenpence a-pound; mutton, tenpence; eggs, eightpence a dozen; and, says my informant, things are now very dear. The people are agricultural, and each one cultivates his little crop. The women are fearfully and wonderfully made; they seem born for hard work, and a large number of the young ones leave yearly for Glasgow, where, as maids-of-all-work, they are much in request. In the mud and rain, children, barefooted, come out to stare. The girls have no bonnets on, the boys mostly wear kilts, but they have all the advantages of a school, and the steamers from Oban now and then bring batches of the Glasgow papers. One of the things that most strikes a stranger in these Western isles is the astonishing number of sweet-shops. Every one is born, it is said, with a sweet tooth in his head, but here every islander must have a dozen at least. Tobermory is no exception to the general rule. The lower part of the town, at the far end of the bay, is chiefly devoted to trade, and at every other shop I see sweets exposed for sale. It is the same at Portree, the capital of Skye, and it is the same at the still more important town of Stornoway, in the island of Lewis. At Tobermory, one sees in the shop windows, besides ship stores, mutton—you never see beef either in the Inner or Outer Hebrides; articles symptomatic of feminine love for fashion —actually a skating-rink hat being one of the attractions at one of the leading shops, though I can't hear of a skating-rink on this side of the world at all. In the interior of the island are farmers and farmers' wives, who evidently have cash to spare. As we skirt along the coast we see here and there a grey castle in ruins, telling of a time and manners and customs long since passed away. At one castle—that of Moy, for instance—the laird was a real knight and chief, and behaved as such. One part of the castle was built over a precipice, and in the wall was a niche in which a man could just stand, and barely that; a man or woman charged with a crime was placed in that niche; after a certain time the door was opened, and if he or she was still standing the result was a verdict of "Not guilty." Had strength or nerve failed, the unhappy individual was considered guilty and had received the punishment due to his or her crime. It was rather hard, this, for weak brethren, and perhaps it is as well that the system is in existence no longer. There was a good deal of the right that is born of might in Scotland then; it is to be hoped that the land is happier now with its castles in ruins, and its sons and daughters wanderers on the face of the earth, farming in Canada, climbing to wealth and power in the United States, governing in India, growing wool in Natal, coming to the front with true Scotch tenacity and instinct everywhere. At the same time, when we need men for our armies and our fleets, and remember that the flower of them come from such islands as Mull, one may regret the forced exile of these hardy sons of the Celt or the Norseman.

VI.

FAST DAY AT PORTREE.

CHAPTER VI.

FAST DAY AT PORTREE.

IN rough weather it requires no little courage to make one's way in a steamer from Tobermory to Portree, the capital of the Isle of Skye. Our noble-hearted owner is very careful on this point. The *Elena* is a beautiful yacht, and he treats her tenderly. It is true, off Ardanamurchan Point we tumble about on the troubled waves of the Atlantic, and are glad to shelter in the quiet harbour of Oronsay, where we pass the night, after the Doctor's lady has gone on shore in search of milk, whilst the Doctor smokes his cigar on the top of the highest spot he can find, and I interview the one policeman of the district, who is unable to put on his official costume, as he tells me it rained heavily yesterday, and his clothes are hung by the fire to dry. At Oronsay there are some six houses, including what is called an hotel. Here and there are some old tubs about us which would cause Mr. Plimsoll's hair to stand on an end, and which seek in this stagnant spot shelter from the gale. Next morning we resume our voyage, leaving Oronsay with a very light heart—to quote a celebrated phrase—and in a few hours are at Portree, after passing the residence of the Macdonald who is a descendant of the Lord of the Isles, and such islands as Rum and Muck, and others with names equally unpoetical in English ears. From afar we watch the giant hills of the Isle of Skye, their summits wreathed in clouds. Mr. Black and Mr. Smith have between them much to answer for. They write of fine weather when the sun shines, when you may see ocean and heaven and earth all alike, serene and beautiful, when the novelty and the beauty of the scene excite wonder and praise and joy. It is then people are glad to come to the Isle of Skye, and find a charm in its lonely and rustic life, in its tranquil lochs and its purple hills; but I fancy in Skye it is as often wet as not; and when we were there the rain was in the ascendant, and one would, except for the name of the thing, have been often just as soon at home. Mr. Spurgeon once said to a Scotchman, as he was pointing out the grandeur of a Highland scene, that it seemed as if God, after He had finished making the world, got together all the spare rubbish, and shot it down there. Apparently something similar has been done with regard to Skye. You are bewildered with their number and variety—rocks to the right, rocks to the left, rocks before, rocks behind, rocks rising steep out of the sea with all sorts of rugged outlines, rocks sloping away into wide moors where no life is to be seen, or into lochs where the fish have it almost all to themselves. It is as well that it should be so. The land does not flow with milk and honey. The hut of a Skye peasant, with its turf walls, its bare and filthy floor, not the sweeter for the fact that the cow—if the owner is rich enough to have one—sleeps behind, its peat fire, with no chimney for the escape of smoke, its bare-legged boys and girls, its sombre men, its gaunt women, seemed to me the climax of human wretchedness.

It is with no common pleasure we get in our boat and are rowed ashore. It is a secular day with us in England. Here, in Portree, it is fast day, and all the shops are closed, and if we had not laid in a stock of mutton at Oronsay, it would have been fast day with us on board the *Elena* as well as with the pious people ashore. It seems to me there are services in the churches, either in English or in Gaelic, all day long. Of course I attend the Gaelic sermon. It is recorded of an old Duke of Argyll that on one occasion he was heard to declare that if he wanted to court a young lady he would talk French, as that was the language of flattery; that if he wished to curse and swear, he would have recourse to English; but that if he wanted to worship God, he would employ the Gaelic tongue. It may be that I heard a bad specimen, as the sermon or service did not seem to be particularly impressive; and as the preacher took a whole hour in which to expound and amplify his text, it must be admitted that, considering I did not understand a word of it, it was not a little wearying. I must, however, own that the people listened with the utmost attention, and that even such of them as were asleep all the time, slept in a quiet, subdued, and reverential manner. Indeed, they think much of religion in this Isle of Skye, and have a profound respect for the clergy. "Sure," said an island guide one day, as he was speaking of a distinguished divine, whom he had attended during a summer tour—"sure he's a verra godly man, he gave me a drink out o' his ain flask." And yet Portree is not a drinking place. There are two or three good hotels for the tourists, and little more. I saw no sign of intoxication on the evening of the fast day, but I did see churches filled, and all business suspended, and the sight of the Gaelic congregation was extremely interesting. The men in good warm home-spun frieze, the women with clean faces, and plaid shawls, and white caps, the younger ones with the last new thing in bonnets, looking as unlike the big, bare-footed damsels of the streets, and the old withered women whom you see coming in from the wide and dreary moor, as it is possible to imagine. In London heresy may prevail—sometimes, it is said, it crosses the Scottish border; but here, at any rate, since the Reformation has flourished the sincere milk of the Word. These men and women have their Gaelic Bible, and that they cling to as their guide in life, their comfort in adversity, their stay and support in death, and as the foundation of their hopes of immortal life and joy. An old gossiping writer, who died a year or two since, relates how a Presbyterian clergyman confessed to him that his congregation, who only used the Gaelic, were so well versed in theology, that it was impossible for him to go beyond their reach in the most profound doctrines of Christianity. Perhaps it is as well for some ministers whom I have heard, but should be sorry to name, that they have not Gaelic hearers. They must be terrible fellows to preach to, these men, fed on the Shorter Catechism, the Proverbs of Solomon, and the rest of the Old and New Testaments. It is little to them what the philosophers think. Mill, and Spencer, and Tyndall, and Huxley they ignore. Dark-eyed, black-haired, with heads which you might knock against a rock without cracking, and with arms and legs that one would fancy could stop the Flying Dutchman,— evidently these are not the men to be tossed about with every wind of doctrine or cunning craftiness of men who lie in wait to deceive. Little pity would they have for the imperfect, weak-kneed brother, who, in the pulpit or out of it, could presume to doubt what they had learnt at their mothers' knees. Up here in Skye, the religion known is bright and clear. The shops are of the poorest description, merely one room in a common dwelling, with a stone or earth floor. There is no paper published in all the Isle of Skye, but the people believe. You man of the nineteenth century, the heir of all the ages underneath the sun, would think little of the peasant of that wintry region. I believe he thinks as little of you as you do of him. You mock, and he believes; you scorn, and he worships; you stammer about Protoplasms and Evolutions, he says in his old Gaelic tongue, "God said, Let there be light, and there was light." There are many in London who would give all that they have if they could believe as these men and women of the North.

There were sermons again in the afternoon, sermons at night, sermons again next day, sermons on the coming Sunday, and to them came the fisher from the sea, the little tradesman from his shop, the ploughman from his croft, the milkmaid from her dairy, and the child from school; and it must further be remembered that these fasts are voluntary, and not in accordance with Acts of Parliament. Remember, also, that nothing is done to make the service attractive. It is simply the usual form of Presbyterian worship that is followed. The chapel was as plain as could be, and the singing was almost funereal. But, after all, the chapel was to be preferred to the empty streets, along which the wind raged like a hurricane, or to the contemplation of bleak rocks and angry seas. I can quite believe at Skye it is more comfortable to go to kirk than stay at home. Indeed, more than once on the night after, I felt perhaps my safest place would have been the kirk, as the wind came rushing in through a gully in the mountains, and kept the water in a constant fury. Really, from the deck of the *Elena,* Portree looked a very comfortable place, with the bay lined with buildings, and conspicuous among them all the Imperial Hotel, where the Empress of the French stayed while travelling in these parts. There is a good deal of excitement here as steamers rush in and out, and yachts lazily drop their anchors. It seems to me that the people quite appreciate the charms of their rocky island. Coming down the cliff, I saw a notice—"Furnished Apartments to Let"—and the price asked was quite conclusive on that head. Down by the harbour an enterprising Scot, who had been a gentleman's servant in London, had established a store for the sale of bottled beer and such pleasant drinks, and seemed quite satisfied with the result of his experiment. At any rate, he preferred Portree to residence further inland, where he said even the very eggs were uneatable, so strongly did they taste of peat. My lady friend—rather, I should say, "our lady"—is as much affected by the gale that dolorous night as myself, and writes, plaintively begging me to excuse the irregularity of the metre on account of the rolling of the vessel, as follows:—

> "Here off Skye,
> The tide runs high;
> Through hill and glen
> Wind howls again.
> The Coolan hills
> No more we see,
> Save through the mists
> Of memory.
> The sea birds float,
> And seem to gloat,
> With loud, shrill note,
> Above our boat;
> For they, like us,
> Are forced to stay
> For shelter in this friendly bay;
> And now I seek, in balmy sleep,
> Oblivion of the perils of the deep,
> And wishing rocks and hills good night,
> Let's hope to-morrow's log will be more bright."

A cottage in the Hebrides is by no means a cottage *ornée*. Its walls are made of stone and clay of a tremendous thickness. On this wall, on a framework of old oars or old wood, are laid large turfs and a roof of thatch. In this roof the fowls nestle, and lay an infinite number of eggs; but all things inside and out are tainted with turf in a way to make them disagreeable. There is no chimney, and but one door, and the floor is the bare earth, with a bench for the family formed of earth or peat or stone. Beds and bedding are unknown. If the family keeps a cow, that has the best corner, for it is what the pig is to the Irishman, the gentleman that pays the rent. Small sheep, almost as horned and hardy as goats, may be met with, but never pigs. Pork seems an abomination in the eyes of the natives. Every cotter has a portion of the adjacent moor in which to cut peat sufficient to supply his wants. Out of the homespun wool the women make good warm garments—and they need them. Fish and porridge seem their principal diet, and it agrees with them. The girls are wonderfully fat and healthy; and consumption is utterly unknown. While I was at Stornoway, an old woman had just died in the workhouse considerably over a century old. As to agricultural operations, they are conducted on a most primitive scale. A few potatoes may here and there be seen struggling for dear life; and as the hay is cut when the sun shines, it is often in August or September that the farmer reaps his scanty harvest. You miss the flowers which hide the deformity of the peasant's cottage in dear old England. It seems altogether in these distant regions, where the wild waves of the Atlantic dash and roar; where the days are dark with cloud; where you see nothing but rock, and glen, and moorland; where forests are an innovation, that man fights with the opposing powers of nature for existence under very great disadvantage.

VII.

TO STORNOWAY.

CHAPTER VII.

TO STORNOWAY.

A FINE day came at last, and we steered off from Portree, leaving the grand Cachullin Mountains, rising to a height of 3,220 feet, and the grave of Flora Macdonald, and the cave where Prince Charles hid himself far behind. On the right were the distant mountains of Ross-shire, and on our left Skye, and the other islands which guard the Western Highlands against the awful storms of the ever-restless Atlantic. Here, as elsewhere, was to be noticed the absence of all human life, whether at sea or on land. It was only now and then we saw a sail, but, as if to compensate for their absence, the birds of the air and the fishes of the sea seemed to follow in a never-ending crowd. More than once we saw a couple of whales spouting and blowing from afar, and the gulls, and divers, and solan-geese at times made the surface of the water absolutely white, like snow-islands floating leisurely along. Just before we got up to Stornoway, at a great distance on our right, Cape Wrath, more than a hundred miles off, lifted up its head into the clear blue sky, the protecting genius, as it were, of the Scottish strand. It was perfectly delightful, this; one felt not only that in Scotland people had at rare intervals fine weather, but that by means of steamers and yachts and sailing vessels of all kinds, the people of Scotland knew how to improve the shining hour. It was beautiful, this floating on a glassy sea, clear as a looking-glass, in which were reflected the clouds, and the skies, and the sun, and the birds of the air, and the rocks, with a wonderful fidelity. It seemed that you had only to plunge into that cool and tempting depth, and to be in heaven at once. At Stornoway we spent a couple of days. The town stands in a bay, perhaps not quite so romantic as some in which we have sheltered, but very picturesque, nevertheless. The first object to be distinctly seen as we entered was the fine castle which Sir James Mathieson has erected for himself, at a cost altogether of half a million, and the grounds of which are in beautiful order; them we had ample time to inspect that evening, as in Stornoway the daylight lasted till nearly ten o'clock. Happily, Sir James was at home, and we on board the yacht had an acceptable present of vegetables, and cream, and butter, very welcome to us poor toilers of the sea. Stornoway is a very busy place, and has at this time of the year a population of 2,500. In May and June it is busier still, as at that time there will be as many as five hundred fishing boats in the harbour, and a large extra population are employed on shore in curing and packing the fish. In the country behind are lakes well stocked with fish, and mountains and moors where game and wild deer and real eagles yet abound. But a great drawback is the climate. An old sportsman writes:—" The savagery of the weather in the Lewes, the island of which Stornoway is the capital, is not to be described. A gentleman from the county of Clare once shot a season with me, and had very good sport, which he enjoyed much. I asked him to come again. 'Not for five thousand pounds a year,' he replied, 'would I encounter this climate again. I am delighted I came, for now I can go back to my own country with pleasure, since, bad as the climate is, it is Elysium to this.'" Let me say, however, the weather was superb all the time the *Elena* was at Stornoway.

As a town, Stornoway is an immense improvement on Portree. It rejoices in churches, and the shops are numerous, and abound with all sorts of useful articles. The chief streets are paved. It has here and there a gas lamp, and the proprietor of the chief hotel boasted to me that so excellent were his culinary arrangements, that actually the ladies from the yachts come and dine there. Stornoway has a Freemasons' Hall, and, wandering in one of the streets, I came to a public library, which I found was open once a week. On Saturday night the shops swarmed with customers, chiefly peasant women—who put their boots on when they came into the town, and who took them off again and walked barefoot as soon as they had left the town behind— and ancient mariners, with a very fish-like smell. On Sunday the churches were full, and at the Free Church, where the service was in Gaelic, the crowd was great. In a smaller church I heard a cousin of Norman Macleod—a fine, burly man—preach a powerful sermon, which seemed to me made up partly of two sermons—one by the late T. T. Lynch, and the other by the late Alfred Morris. I strayed also into a U. P. church, but there, alas! the audience was small. In Stornoway, as elsewhere, the couplet is true—

" The free kirk, the poor kirk, the kirk without the steeple,
The auld kirk, the rich kirk, the kirk without the people."

On the Monday morning we turned our faces homeward, and as the weather was fine, we passed outside Skye, and saw Dunvegan Bay, of which Alexander Smith writes so much; passing rocky islands, all more or less known to song, and caves with dark legends of blood, and cruelty, and crime. One night was spent in Bunessan Bay, where some noble sportsmen were very needlessly, but, *con amore*, butchering the few peaceful seals to be found in those parts; and a short while we lay off Staffa, which rises straight out of the water like an old cathedral, where the winds and waves ever play a solemn dirge. In its way, I know nothing more sublime than Staffa, with its grey arch and black columns and rushing waves. No picture or photograph I have seen ever can give any adequate idea of it. "Altogether," writes Miss Gordon Cumming, " it is a scene of which no words can convey the smallest idea;" and for once I agree with the lady. It is seldom the reality surpasses your expectations. As regards myself, in the case of Staffa I must admit it did.

The same morning we land at Columba, or the Holy Isle. The story of St. Columba's visit to Iona is laid somewhere in the year A.D. 563. He, it seems, according to some authorities, was an Irishman, and from Iona he and his companions made the tour of Pagan Scotland; and hence now Scotland is true blue Presbyterian and always Protestant. Here, as at Staffa, we miss the tourists, who scamper and chatter for an hour at each place, and then are off; and I was glad. As Byron writes :—

> " I love not man the less, but nature more,
> From these our interviews, in which I steal
> From all I may be or have been before,
> To mingle with the universe, and feel
> What I can ne'er express, yet cannot all conceal."

The history of Iona is a history of untold beauty and human interest. Druids, Pagans, Christian saints, have all inhabited the Holy Isle. Proud kings, like Haco of Norway, were here consecrated, and here—

> " Beneath the showery west,
> The mighty kings of three fair realms were laid."

All that I could do was to visit the ruins of the

monastery and the cathedral, and one of the stone crosses, of which there were at one time 360, and to regret that these beautiful monoliths were cast into the sea by the orders of the Synod as "monuments of idolatrie." St. Columba, like all the saints, was a little ungallant as regards the fair sex. Perhaps it is as well that his rule is over. He would not allow even cattle on the sacred isle. "Where there is a cow," argued the saint, "there must be a woman; and where there is a woman there must be mischief." Clearly, the ladies have very much improved since the lamented decease of the saint. From Iona we made our way to the very prosperous home of commerce and whisky known as Campbeltown. Actually, the duty on the latter article paid by the Campbeltown manufacturers amounts to as much as £60,000 a year. At one time it was the very centre of Scottish life. For three centuries it was the capital of Scotland. It is still a very busy place, and it amused me much of a night to watch the big, bare-footed, bare-headed women crowding round the fine cross in the High Street, which ornaments what I suppose may be called the Parochial Pump. Close to the town is the church and cave of St. Kieran, the Apostle of Cantyre, the tutor of St. Columba. At present the chief boast of Campbeltown is that there were born the late Norman Macleod and Burns' Highland Mary. When Macleod was a boy the days of smuggling were not yet over in that part of the world. Here is one of his stories:—" Once an old woman was being tried before the Sheriff, and it fell to his painful duty to sentence her. 'I dare say,' he said uneasily to the culprit, 'it is not often you have fallen into this fault.' 'No, indeed, shura,' was the reply; 'I hae na made a drap since yon wee keg I sent yoursel'.'" Let me remark, *en passant*, that my friend, the Doctor, was born here, and that is proof positive that at Campbeltown the breed of great men is not yet exhausted. I mention this to our lady, and she is of the same opinion.

VIII.

KINTYRE AND CAMPBELTOWN.

CHAPTER VIII.

KINTYRE AND CAMPBELTOWN.

In my wanderings in the latter town I pick up the last edition of a useful and unpretending volume called "The History of Kintyre," by Mr. Peter M'Intosh — a useful citizen who carried on the profession of a catechist, and who is now no more. The book has merits of its own, as it shows how much may be done by any ordinary man of average ability who writes of what he has seen and heard. Kintyre is a peninsula on the extreme south of the shire of Argyle, in length about forty geographical miles. That the Fingalians occasionally resided at Kintyre is without doubt, and a description of their bravery and generosity is graphically given in some of the poems of Ossian. At one time there was much wood in its lowlands, and in them were elk, deer, wild boars, &c., and the rivers abounded with fish. There were clans who gathered together with the greatest enthusiasm around their chiefs, who repaired to a high hill, and set up a large fire on the top of it, in full view of the surrounding district, each unfolding his banner, ensign, or pennant, his pipers playing appropriate tunes. The clan got into motion, repaired to their chief like mountain streams rushing into the ocean. He eloquently addressed them in the heart-stirring language of the Gael, and, somewhat like a Kaffir chief of the present day, dwelt at length on the heroism of his ancestors. The will of the chief instantly became law, and preparations were soon made; the chief in his uniform of clan tartan takes the lead, the pipers play well-known airs, and the men follow, their swords and spears glittering in the air.

Up to very recent times there were those who remembered this state of things. An old man who died not a century ago told my informant, writes Mr. M'Intosh, that the first thing he ever recollected was a great struggle between his father and his mother in consequence of the father preparing to join his clan in a bloody expedition. The poor wife exerted all her strength, moral and physical, but in vain. He left her never to return alive from the battle-field. The proprietors of Kintyre were wise in their generation, and mustered men in their different districts to oppose Prince Charles, partly on account of his religion, and partly to retain their lands. On one occasion they marched to Falkirk, but not in time to join in the battle, it being over before they reached there. Prince Charles being victorious, they went into a church, which the Highlanders surrounded, coming in with their clothes dyed with blood, and crying out " Massacre them "; but they were set at liberty on the ground that their hearts were with the Prince, and had been compelled by their chiefs to take arms on the side of the House of Hanover against their will. But even the chiefs were not always masters, and men often did that which was right in their own eyes alone. An instance of this kind is traditionally told about the Black Fisherman of Lochsanish. The loch, which is now drained, was a mile in length and half-a-mile in breadth, and contained a great number of salmon and trout. The Black Fisherman would not suffer any person to live in the neighbourhood, but claimed, by the strength of his arm, sole dominion over the loch. The Chief Largie, who lived eighteen miles north of the loch, kept a guard of soldiers, lest the Fisherman should make an attack on him. He sent his soldiers daily to Balergie Cruach to see if the Fisherman was on the loch fishing, and if they saw him fishing they would come home, not being afraid of an attack on that day. A stranger one day coming to Largie's house asked him why he kept soldiers. The answer was, it was on account of the Fisherman. When he saw him sitting he went and fought the Fisherman, bidding the soldiers wait the result on a neighbouring hill. When the battle was over, the Fisherman was minus his head. We read the head, which was very heavy, was left at Largie's door. These old men were always fighting. The number of large stones we see erected in different parts of Kintyre have been set up in memory of battles once fought at these places. On one occasion two friendly clans prepared to come and meet. They met somewhere north of Tarbert, but did not know each other, and began to ask their names, which in those days it was considered cowardice to answer. They drew swords, fought fiercely, and killed many on both sides. At last they found out their mistake, were very, very sorry, and, after burying their dead, returned to their respective places. The feuds and broils among the clans were frequent, and really for the most trifling causes, as the whole clans always stood by their chiefs, and were ready at a moment's notice to fight on account of any insult, real or imaginary. It appears that in this distant part of the Empire, though the whole district is not far from Glasgow, with its commerce and manufactures, and university and newspapers, and the modern Athens, with its great literary traditions, there still linger many old Druid superstitions.

Some are particularly interesting. Old M'Intosh thus writes of May-day and the first of November, called in Gaelic Bealtuinn, or Beil-teine, signifying Belus fire, and Samhuinn, or serene time.

On the first of May the Druids kindled a large fire on the top of a mountain, from which a good view of the horizon might be seen, that they might see the sun rising; the inhabitants of the whole country assembling, after extinguishing their fire, in order to welcome the rising sun and to worship God. The chief Druid, blessing the people and receiving their offerings, gave a kindling to each householder. If the Druid was displeased at any of the people, he would not give him a kindling; and no other person was allowed to give it, on pain of being cursed, and being unfortunate all the year round. This superstition is observed by some to this day. On the first of November the Druids went nearly through the same ceremony.

The superstition of wakes in Kintyre is nearly worn out. The origin of this superstition is, that when one died the Druid took charge of his soul, conveying it to Flath-innis, or heaven; but the friends of the deceased were to watch, or wake, the body, lest the evil spirits should take it away, and leave some other substance in its place. When interred, it could never be removed.

An old man named John M'Taggart, who died long ago, was owner of a fine little smack, with which he trafficked from Kintyre to Ireland and other places. Being anxious to get a fair wind to go to Ireland, and hearing of an old woman who pretended to have the power to give this, he made a bargain with her. She gave him two strings with three knots on each; when he undid the first, he got a fine fair breeze; getting into mid-channel he opened the second, and got a strong gale; and when near the Irish shore he wished to see the effect of the third knot, which, when he loosed, a great hurricane blew, which destroyed some of the houses on shore. With the other string he came back to Kintyre, only opening two of the knots. The old man believed in this superstition.

On the island of Gigha is a well with some stones in it, and it is said that if the stones be taken out of it a great storm will arise. Two or three old men told M'Intosh that they opened the well, and that a fearful storm arose, and they would swear to it if pressed to confirm their belief; they would affirm also to the existence of the Brunie in Cara.

In Carradale is a hill called Sroin-na-h-eana-chair, in which it is said an old creature resides from generation to generation, who makes a great noise before the death of individuals of a certain clan. An old man with whom M'Intosh conversed on the subject declared that he had heard the cries himself, which made the whole glen tremble.

A little dwarf, called the "Caointeach," or weeper, is said to weep before the death of some persons. Some people thought this supernatural creature very friendly. An old wife affirmed that she saw the little creature, about the size of a new-born infant, weep with the voice of a young child, and shortly afterwards got notice of the death of a friend. Others affirmed that they heard the trampling of people outside of the house at night, and shortly after a funeral left the house. Many stories are told about apparitions in the hearing of the young, making an impression which continues all their days. Peter the Catechist deprecates such conduct. He writes: " I have seen those who would not turn on their heel to save their life on the battle-field, who would tremble at the thought of passing alone a place said to be frequented by a spirit."

Very provokingly he next observes, " It would be ridiculous to speak of the charms, omens, gestures, dreams, &c." Now, the fact is, it is just these things which are matters of interest to an inquiring mind. They are absurdities to us, but they were not so once; and then comes the question, Why? He does, however, add a little to our fund of information relative to the second sight.

" An old man who lived at Crossibeg, four generations ago, saw visions, which were explained to him by a supernatural being, descriptive of future events in Kintyre. An account of them was printed, and entitled 'Porter's Prophecies,' which I have perused, but cannot tell if any of them have come to pass as yet, but some people believed them.

"The Laird of Caraskie, more than a century ago, is said to have had a familiar spirit called Beag-bheul, or little mouth, which talked to him, and took great care of him and his property. The spirit told him of a great battle which would be fought in Kintyre, and that the magpie would drink human blood from off a standing stone erected near Campbeltown. The stone was removed, and set as a bridge over the mill water, over which I have often traversed; but the battle has not been fought as yet, and perhaps never will be.

"The Rev. Mr. Boes, a minister of Campbeltown, more than a century ago, was said to have the second sight. One time being at the Assembly, and coming home on Saturday to preach to his congregation, he was overtaken by a storm, which drove the packet into Rothesay. He went to preach in the church on the Sabbath. The rafters of the church above not being lathed, in the middle of his sermon he looked up, and with a loud voice cried, 'Ye're there, Satan; ye kept me from preaching to my own congregation, but ye cannot keep me from preaching for all that,' and then went on with his sermon. At another time, his congregation having assembled on the Sabbath as usual, the minister was walking rapidly on the grass after the time of meeting, the elders not being willing to disturb him by telling him the time was expired. At last he clapped his hands, exclaiming, 'Well done, John;' the Duke of Argyle being at that moment at the head of the British army in Flanders fighting a battle in which he was victorious. The minister, by the power of the second sight, witnessed the battle, and exclaimed, when he saw it won, 'Well done, John.' He went afterwards and preached to his congregation.

"Another Sabbath, when preaching, a member of the congregation having fallen asleep, he cried to him 'Awake.' In a short time the man fell asleep again. The minister bade him awake again and hear the sermon. The man fell asleep the third time, when the minister cried, with a loud voice, 'Awake, and hear this sermon, for it will be the last you will ever hear in this life.' Before the next Sabbath the man was dead. On the morning of a Communion Sabbath, Mr. Boes got up very early, convinced that something was wrong about the church. He examined it, and found that the beams of the gallery were almost sawn through by the emissaries of Satan, in order that the congregation, by the falling of the gallery, might be killed. He got carpenters and smiths employed till they put the church in a safe state, and proceeded with the solemn service of the day with great earnestness. Mr. Boes was sometimes severely tried with temptations, having imaginary combats with Satan, and, being very ill-natured, he would not allow any person to come near him. On one of these occasions he shut himself up in his room for three days. His wife being afraid he would starve with hunger, sent the servant-man with food to him, but the minister scattered it on the floor. The servant-man exclaimed, 'The devil's in the man!' In a moment the minister, becoming calm, answered, 'You are quite right,' then partook of the food, and returned to his former habits."

The following is a good illustration of an olden chief :—We have many traditional stories about

Saddell Castle, in which Mr. M'Donald or "Righ Fionghal" resided. He claimed despotic power over the inhabitants of Kintyre. It is said he knew the use of gunpowder, and often made a bad use of it. He would for sport shoot people, though they did him no harm, with his long gun, which was kept in Carradale for a long time after his death. His character is represented as being very tyrannical. Being once in Ireland, he saw a beautiful married woman, whom he fancied, and took away from her husband to Saddell. Her husband followed; but M'Donald finding him, intended to have starved him to death without his wife knowing it. He was put in a barn, but he kept himself alive by eating the corn which he found there. M'Donald removed him to another place, but a hen came in every day and kept him alive with her eggs. M'Donald was anxious that the poor man should die, and placed him in another place, where he got nothing to eat, and it is said the miserable prisoner ate his own hand, then his arm to the elbow, before he died, and said, in Gaelic, "Dh'ith mi mo choig meoir a's mo lamh gu'm uilleann. Is mor a thig air neach nach eiginu fhulang." When they were burying him, his wife was on the top of the castle, and asked whose funeral it was; she was told it was Thomson's. "Is it my Thomson?" she inquired. "Yes," they replied. She then said they might stop for a little till she would be with them. She immediately threw herself over the castle wall, and was carried dead with her husband to the same grave.

Perhaps, after all, Saxon rule has not been such an injury to the Western Isles of Scotland as some people think. At Kintyre there are plenty of schools, and parsons and policemen instead of robber chiefs; and if there are few freebooting expeditions to Ireland and elsewhere, it is quite as well that people have taken to a more decent mode of life.

Alas! my "to-morrow"—unlike that of the poet, which "never comes"—is at hand. Under a smiling sky, and on a summer sea, we thread our way past Arran, or the Land of Sharp Pinnacles, down the Kyles of Bute, where the scenery is of exquisite beauty; past Rothesay, the Hastings of the West, and with an aquarium said to be the finest in the world, and almost as flourishing as that Hastings of the South which rejoices in a yatchsman for M.P. of unrivalled fame; past Dunoon, till we drop anchor at

Hunters' Quay. We seem all at once to have come into the world again. On every side of us there are steamers bearing tourists, and holiday-makers, and health-seekers to the crowded bathing-places and health resorts. As we approach our journey's end, the Clyde seems covered with rowing-boats, and music and laughter echo along its waters. I feel a little sad to think that my brief holiday is over. The Doctor and the Doctor's lady tell me we shall meet in London, and that is a consolation. Yes, we shall meet, but no more as equals on deck. He will be in the pulpit or on the platform, I beneath. There is no equality when a man puts on the black gown, and begins lecturing to the pew. The mutual standpoint vanishes like a dream. But when, oh, when shall I sail in such a model yacht as the *Elena* again, or meet with such hospitality as I enjoyed at its worthy owner's hands? His sons, amphibious as are all the Scotchmen, apparently, in these parts, row out to meet us. The greeting is as affectionate as mostly the greetings of the British race are. "What did you come back for? We were gettting on very well without you," were the first words I heard.

IX.

BACK AGAIN.

CHAPTER IX.

BACK AGAIN.

As next morning I crossed the Clyde, and took my seat in a crowded and early train, it seemed to me that rain was not far off, and that at Edinburgh Royalty might be favoured with a sight of what in England is known as Scotch mist. Nor were my forebodings wrong. The modern Athens was under a cloud, and many were the heavy-hearted who had come from far and near to do honour to the day. The Glasgow men have but a poor opinion of the citizens of Edinburgh. They took a very unfavourable view of the matter. If Edinburgh desired to have a statue of Albert the Good, why not? If the Queen liked to be present at its inauguration, there was no harm in that; if there were a little fuller ceremonial on the occasion, it was only what was to be expected; but that Edinburgh should hasten to wash her statues and decorate her streets; that she should clean up her shopfronts, and drape her balconies; that she should devote a day to holiday-making; that she should go to the expense of Venetian masts and scarlet cloth—in short, that in this way Edinburgh should attempt to rival a London Lord Mayor's Show, was one of those things no Glasgow fellow could understand.

And I own at first sight there seemed to be a good deal in the Glasgow criticism. Few cities have so fair a site as the noble metropolis of our northern brethren; few cities less require ornamentation. Hers emphatically is that beauty which unadorned is adorned the most. To stand in Princes Street, with the castle frowning on you on one side, and with the Calton Hill in front; to loiter under the fair memorial to Sir Walter Scott (by the side of which I am pleased to see a statue of Livingstone has just been placed); to look from the bridge which connects the New Town with the Old —on the distant hills and the blue sea beyond —is a pleasure in itself. With its far-reaching associations, with its memories of Wilson and Brougham, and Jeffery and Walter Scott, with its dark churches, in which John Knox thundered away at the fair and frail Mary, with its ancient palaces grim and venerable with stirring romance or startling crime, it seemed almost profane to send for the upholsterer, and to bid him deck out the streets and squares with gaudy colours and gay flowers. When on Thursday the morning opened cloudily on the scene, it seemed as if all this preparation had been thrown away; and bright eyes were for awhile dark and sad, and refusing to be comforted. However, the thing went on, nevertheless. The crowd turned out into the streets, the railways brought their tens of thousands from far and near; balconies were full, and all the windows; and the sight was one such as has not feasted the eyes of the oldest inhabitant for many a year. There were the soldiers to line the streets, there were the archers to guard the daïs, there were the Town Council and Lord Provost in their scarlet robes, there were the men whom Edinburgh delights to honour all before them, and, above all, the Duke of Connaught, the Princess Beatrice, Prince Leopold, Brown—the far-famed Highlander—and the Queen. The ceremony itself was not long. When Charlotte Square was reached, Her Majesty took the place assigned to her, and the work was speedily performed. As

Her Majesty went back by Princes Street, an additional interest was created, and Princes Street looked very well; its hotels and fashionable shops rejoiced in crimson and yellow banners, and the Walter Scott memorial even broke out in honour of the day. It was decorated with flags, which waved gaily in the sun—for the sun did come out, after all. But Princes Street was not the chief route. It was down George Street that Royalty drove, and it was there that the efforts of the decorative artist had been most effective. Some of them were very beautiful, and full of taste; but the lettering was rather small. Nor did the inscriptions display much ingenuity. They were mostly "Welcomes," or invitations to "Come again." It was the advertising tradesmen who were most ingenious in that way, and it was in the papers that their efforts appeared. As, for instance, an enterprising shoemaker writes :—

"Welcome, Victoria! Queen of Scottish hearts!
In many a breast the loyal impulse starts"—

and then finishes with a recommendation of his boots and shoes. As a crowd, also, it must be noted that the mob was far graver than a London one, and that little attempt was made either to relieve the tedium of waiting the arrival of the procession, or to turn a penny by the sale of the various articles which seem invariably to be required by a London mob. The boys who sell the evening papers, one would have thought, would have had correct programmes of the procession, and portraits of the Queen and Prince Albert to dispose of. As it was, all that was hawked about was an engraving of the statue itself.

As to the statue, it will be one of the many for which Edinburgh is famous, and at present, as the latest, is considered one of the best. It is in a good position in Charlotte Square—the finest of the Edinburgh squares—and stands by itself. Afar off is William Pitt; and, further off still, unfortunately for the morals of Albert the Good, who is placed just by, is George the Magnificent, swaggering in his cloak, in tipsy gravity, as it were; and at St. Andrew's Square, at the other end, proudly towers above all the Melville Monument. That was utilised on the day in question in an admirable manner— Venetian masts were erected at the end of the grass-plat which surrounds it. Ropes rich with bunting were suspended between them and the statue, which was gaily decked with flags. It was in this neighbourhood, and as you went on to Holyrood, that the ornaments were of the richest character. Of the sixty designs submitted to the committee, the preference was given to that of Mr. John Steell, R.S.A., who was subsequently knighted by Her Majesty. It was on the occasion of the great Volunteer review in the Queen's Park, in 1861, that Prince Albert was seen by the largest number of Scotch people; and it has evidently been the aim of the artist to represent him as he was then—in his uniform of field-marshal, with his cocked hat in his right hand, while he holds the reins in his left. The princely rank of the wearer is indicated by an order on the left breast. In order that the representation might be as perfect as possible, Her Majesty lent the artist the very uniform worn on the occasion referred to. The modelling of the busts was also done at Windsor Castle, under Royal supervision. The horse was modelled from one lent by the Duke of Buccleugh. On the pedestal are bas-reliefs indicative of the character and pursuits of His Royal Highness. On one side his marriage is represented; on another his visit to the International Exhibition. Again we see him peacefully happy at home in the bosom of his family; then again as a rewarder of the merit he was ever anxious to discover and befriend. In one part of the design are quotations from the Prince's speeches, and classical emblems; rank and wealth and talent, in all phases of society, down to the very lowest, are represented as uniting to do honour to the dead. In this varied work Mr. Steell was assisted, at his own request, by Mr. William Brodie, Mr. Clark Stanton, and the late Mr. MacCallum, whose unfinished work was completed by Mr. Stevenson. The equestrian figure is upwards of fourteen feet high, and weighs about eight tons. The pedestal is of five blocks of Peterhead granite. According to a contemporary, the Queen's emotion was manifest when the statue was unveiled. The Scotch are a cautious people, and are very slow in expressing an opinion on the memorial. All I can say is, that I prefer it very much to that statue at the commencement of the Holborn Viaduct, on which Mr. Meeking's young men look down every day.

It was on the next day that you saw the statue and the preparations to the most advantage, and such seemed to be the opinion of all Edinburgh and the surrounding country. A cloudless sky and an Indian sun tinted everything with gold, and a smart breeze set all the flags of the Venetian masts waving all along the line in a way at once effective and bewildering. Fashionable people filled up the streets, dashing equipages drove rapidly past, shops were crammed, waiters at the hotels were tired to death. I never saw so many hungry Scots as I did at a celebrated restaurant, and a hungry Scot is not a pleasant sight; and at the railway station I question whether half the people got into their right carriages after all. Porters and guards seemed alike confused; and the people walked up and down the platform of the Waverley Station as sheep without a shepherd. However, wearied and hungry and bewildered as they were, they had had a day's pleasure, and that was enough.

As for myself I took the Waverley route, and gliding past the ruins of Craig Millar Castle—the prison-house of James the Fifth, and the favourite residence of Queen Mary—and vainly trying to catch a view of Abbotsford, of which one can see but the waving woods, was gratified with a glimpse of Melrose, where rests the heart of Bruce, which the Douglas had vainly striven to carry to Palestine. All round me are names and places connected with border tradition and song. Dryburgh Abbey is not far off, nor Hazeldean, nor Minto House. Passing along the banks of the Teviot, by the frowning heights of Rubertslaw on the left, I reach Hawick, whose history abounds in heroic tale and legendary lore, although the present town is now only known as an important and flourishing emporium of the woollen manufactures. Passing up the vale of the Slitrig, famous in legendary story, we come to Stobs Castle and Branxholme House, celebrated in the " Lay of the Last Minstrel." Close by is Hermitage Castle, founded by Comyn, Earl of Monteith, where Lord de Soulis was boiled as a reputed sorcerer at a Druidical spot, named the Nine Stane Rig, at the head of the glen. At Kershope Foot the railway, having passed through the land of the Armstrongs, renowned in border warfare, enters England. Once more I am at home, thankful to have seen so much of beauty and blessedness, of wonders in heaven above, and on the earth beneath, and in the waters underneath the earth ; thankful also for improved health and power of work acquired by yachting among the islands of the Western Coast.

MIDLAND RAILWAY.

Improved and Accelerated Service of
NEW EXPRESS TRAINS
BETWEEN
ENGLAND & SCOTLAND
BY THE
SETTLE AND CARLISLE ROUTE.

The SUMMER SERVICE of EXPRESS TRAINS between LONDON (St. Pancras) and SCOTLAND is now in operation, and Express Trains leave St. Pancras for Scotland at 5.15 and 10.30 a.m., and at 8.0 and 9.15 p.m. on Week-Days, and at 9.15 p.m. only on Sundays.

A new NIGHT EXPRESS TRAIN now leaves St. Pancras for Edinburgh and Perth at 8 p.m. on Week-Days, arriving at Perth at 8.40 a.m., in connection with Trains leaving Perth for Montrose and Aberdeen at 9.20 a.m., and for Inverness and Stations on the Highland Railway at 9.30 a.m.

A new Night Express in connection with the Train leaving Inverness at 12.40 p.m., Aberdeen at 4.5 p.m., and Dundee at 6.30 p.m., leaves Perth at 7.25 p.m., and Edinburgh at 10.30 p.m. on Week-Days, arriving at St. Pancras at 8.30 a.m.

A PULLMAN SLEEPING CAR is run between ST. PANCRAS and PERTH in each direction by these Trains.

Pullman Sleeping Cars are also run from St. Pancras to Edinburgh and Glasgow by the Night Express leaving London at 9.15 p.m.; and from Edinburgh and Glasgow to St. Pancras by the Express leaving Edinburgh at 9.20 p.m., and Glasgow at 9.15 p.m. on Week-Days and Sundays. Pullman Drawing-Room Cars are run between the same places by the Day Express Trains leaving St. Pancras for Edinburgh and Glasgow at 10.30 a.m., and Glasgow at 10.15 a.m., and Edinburgh at 10.30 a.m. for St. Pancras.

These Cars are well ventilated, fitted with Lavatory, &c., accompanied by a special attendant, and are *unequalled for comfort and convenience* in travelling.

The 9.15 p.m. Express from St. Pancras reaches Greenock in ample time for passengers to join the "Iona" steamer.

Tourist Tickets, available for two months, are issued from St. Pancras and all principal stations on the Midland Railway to Edinburgh, Glasgow, Greenock, Oban (by "Iona" steamer from Greenock), and other places of tourist resort in all parts of Scotland.

The Passenger Fares and the Rates for Horses and Carriages between stations in England and stations in Scotland have been revised and considerably reduced by the opening of the Midland Company's Settle and Carlisle Route.

Guards in charge of the Through Luggage and of Passengers travelling between London and Edinburgh and Glasgow by the Day and Night Express Trains in each direction.

Derby, August, 1877.   JAMES ALLPORT, *General Manager.*

GLASGOW and the HIGHLANDS.

THE ROYAL MAIL STEAMERS,
(Royal Route viâ Crinan and Caledonian Canals)

Iona,	Linnet,	Islay,
Chevalier,	Cygnet,	Clydesdale,
Gondolier,	Plover,	Clansman,
Mountaineer,	Staffa,	Lochawe,
Pioneer,	Glencoe,	Lochiel,
Glengarry,	Inverary Castle,	Lochness,

and Queen of the Lake,

Sail during the season for Islay, Oban, Fort-William, Inverness, Staffa, Iona, Lochawe, Glencoe, Tobermory, Portree, Gairloch, Ullapool, Lochinver, and Stornoway; affording Tourists an opportunity of visiting the magnificent scenery of Glencoe, the Coolin Hills, Loch Coruisk, Loch Maree, and the famed Islands of Staffa and Iona.

Time Bill with Maps free by post on application to DAVID HUTCHESON & CO., 119, Hope-street, Glasgow.

www.ingramcontent.com/pod-product-compliance
Lightning Source LLC
Chambersburg PA
CBHW020142170426
43199CB00010B/853